Original title:

The Pot and the Poet

Copyright © 2025 Creative Arts Management OÜ
All rights reserved.

Author: Olivia Sterling
ISBN HARDBACK: 978-1-80581-721-5
ISBN PAPERBACK: 978-1-80581-248-7
ISBN EBOOK: 978-1-80581-721-5

A Connection of Craft and Heart

In a shop where clay spins fast,
A jester molds with a chuckle and cast.
Lumpy shapes that wobble and twirl,
His artistic dreams all start to unfurl.

With a pinch and a poke, he gives it a grin,
A silly vase with a goofy spin.
It wobbles and jiggles, a sight to behold,
A masterpiece crafted, with stories untold.

He laughs at the clay that just won't behave,
Thinking it smarter than the whims he gave.
But in every blunder, a treasure might hide,
Wit and charm found in each joyful slide.

Fired with laughter, his funny designs,
Invite all the folks to share in the signs.
For every crack and every odd shape,
A silly connection, an artistic escape.

The Dialogue of Earth and Expression

In the garden where dreams take root,
A figure stands with a quirky flute.
The soil giggles, it knows it's true,
Planting laughs, not just a few.

Words sprout like weeds in sunny weather,
Dance around, oh what a tether!
A chat with dirt on what to say,
As flowers grin, in bright array.

Spirals of Thought in a Tongue of Clay

A lump of clay, a brain in twirl,
It twists and turns, oh watch it whirl.
Expressions oozing, like ice cream's drip,
In giggles and glee, they take a trip.

A mold for laughter, a cup for cheer,
Each swirl tells tales that we hold dear.
With every pinch, a tale to tell,
Even the baker's yeast laughs as well.

Shaping the Unseen with Similes

Metaphors swirl like sugarplum dreams,
They tickle the thoughts with whimsical beams.
A potter shapes thoughts, oh what a mess,
Slipping on words, in a playful dress.

With every poke, a chuckle breaks free,
Imagining what the world could be.
As puns take shape, and witticisms flow,
The clay just giggles, putting on a show.

Visions Forged in Ashes and Verses

From old tales, fiery as the sun,
Ashes whisper of mischief and fun.
The poet's quill, a magic wand,
Bends the rules of the mundane land.

Verses flutter like butterflies bright,
Lighting up shadows, igniting delight.
A wagging tongue, a flick of the wrist,
Turns ashes to laughter, none could resist.

Emotions Shaped in Tangible Form

A lump of clay that sits and sighs,
It giggles as it twists and tries.
With every mold, a vision turns,
A heart that laughs, a spirit yearns.

In every spin, a dance takes flight,
With silly shapes that feel just right.
A bowl, a jug, a goofy face,
Where joy and laughter find their place.

Lines Surrendered to the Craft

The ink flows free, a wild parade,
Each word a jester, unafraid.
With playful rhymes that bounce and bop,
They hop and skip, they never stop.

A line that slips, a pun unrolls,
As laughter spills from heart and souls.
In every curve, the humor lies,
A punchline found 'neath cloudy skies.

The Shaping of Eloquent Silences

In quiet corners, laughter brews,
As silence fills with playful clues.
Shapes emerge, both round and odd,
In silent jest, a cheeky nod.

A tilt, a turn, a wink to share,
In a still moment, jokes declare.
The unspoken giggles softly hum,
In silence, too, there's joy to come.

Poetic Transformations in Fired Earth

A fiery kiln, a spark of joy,
Transforming clay, a cheeky toy.
From basic blob to funky art,
In every crack, a laugh can start.

The heat ignites a clever grin,
As masterpieces slowly spin.
Through molten dreams, hilarity flows,
A quirk in form, as humor grows.

Elegy of Shards and Sonnets

In the corner a jar did dwell,
With tales of mishaps it could tell.
A slip of hand, oh what a mess,
Fractured dreams in ceramic dress.

The poet chuckled at the sight,
As pieces twinkled in the light.
A sonnet formed from broken clay,
Laughter ruled the fractured play.

Songs of the Hearth and Hands

At the hearth where stories blend,
A potter's wheel, a loyal friend.
With clay beneath now spinning round,
The music of the soil is found.

Hands are busy, tensions flee,
While songs escape, wild and free.
A cup appears, but what's this shape?
A funny mug of new escape!

Muddy Hands and Inked Soul

Muddy hands in playful cheer,
Stroking clay, no need to fear.
Inked soul sings of joy's embrace,
As smudges paint a smiling face.

Each twist, each turn, a giggle bright,
Crafting wonders day and night.
But wait—a cup that can't quite stand,
A wobbly joke from skilled hands!

Crafters of Worlds

In the studio, worlds collide,
With whimsy flowing like a tide.
Shaping dreams with every spin,
Laughter echoes, let's begin!

A strange vase that seems to grin,
Adorning shelves with cheeky spin.
Crafters chuckled at each flaw,
Worlds constructed with awe and guffaw.

Wordsmiths of Clay

Wordsmiths shaping lines like clay,
Turning phrases in a playful way.
With every twist, a line emerges,
Humor flows as laughter surges.

A pot that rhymes, a mug that sings,
In the workshop, joy that clings.
The scribe and potter in delight,
Crafting laughter day and night.

Poetry in Porcelain

A bowl sat there, shiny and bright,
I thought it could hold my thoughts, what a sight!
I poured in my dreams, quite a lot,
But it cracked with laughter, oh what a plot!

Each cup that I made, wobbled and swayed,
The tea spilled out, oh what a parade!
My rhymes slipped away, like sugar on tea,
The dishes just chuckled, all mocking of me!

Fables in Firing Flames

Once there was clay, so soft and so bold,
I shaped a tall tale, or so I was told.
But under the heat, my story did bend,
Like my bright new vase, it soon met its end!

With every crackle, my laughter ignites,
What a spectacle! Such comical sights!
The fables I told melted into a stew,
And the flames just hummed, 'What's next to pursue?'

The Art of Shaping Tales

I plied a fine tale with my nimble hands,
Thought it would rival great writer's grand plans.
But alas! It was squished, a pancake so flat,
My audience roared, 'What's that? Oh, what's that?'

I sculpted my stories with whimsy and cheer,
But my jug had a mind, it ran off with a beer!
The art of my craft now a funny old game,
As my tales take flight, and my vessels get fame!

Echoes of Creativity

Echoes arose from the kiln's warm embrace,
'That rhyme we just fired, oh, where is its place?'
In a dance of clay, laughter filled the air,
As the artwork jiggled, without a care!

The echoes a-jesting, from bowl to the mug,
They chattered and giggled, well snug as a bug.
Creativity's laughter rolled round in a spree,
A gallery of gabs, all shaped joyfully!

Spiral Paths of Ink and Clay

In a world where clay can talk,
A jug shared jokes with a block of rock.
The ink, it giggled on the page,
While molds tapped dance on the stage.

A bowl once tried to write a rhyme,
But ended up with soup each time.
The spatula laughed, what a great scene,
As pots flung words like a machine!

A plate once claimed it was a star,
But only shone from the kitchen jar.
A cup said, 'Let's stir up some fun!'
While spoons aligned, ready to run.

In this realm of twist and shout,
Each vessel boasts, without a doubt.
Clay and ink, in giggles play,
Creating chaos in a fray.

Clay Echoes Translated into Verse

An urn spilled secrets none could trust,
While teapots giggled, adding rust.
A mug declared it was so wise,
But poured out truth with silly lies.

Pans were plotting in the night,
Hatching schemes for a food fight.
"Let's mix some phrases!" they would cheer,
As culinary dreams drew near.

A pitcher poured out tales of woe,
Of crumbs that danced and stole the show.
With whiskers twitching, spoons did cheer,
"More spice, more fun, let's volunteer!"

In this echo of clay's embrace,
Every dish smiled with a face.
Translation of laughter in every curve,
Crafted stories not meant to conserve.

Sculpting the Invisible with Language

Words like clay, in hands that mold,
Sculpted laughter, warm and bold.
A metaphor glided on a spoon,
While similes hummed a happy tune.

Narratives danced on the edge of a plate,
As utensils sang, oh, what a fate!
"Catch the rhymes before they slip!"
With spatulas joining in every quip.

Jokes were formed in a mixing bowl,
As the chef poet took a stroll.
The invisible outlined in flour,
While forks juggled during the hour.

With language swirling in the air,
Each twist and turn showed how we care.
In this art, so joyous and bright,
Clay and laughs took fervent flight.

The Art of Breath between Fingers

Fingers dusted with dreams and clay,
Crafting thoughts that seem to sway.
An oven hummed a silly tune,
While lights danced around like a moon.

A pinch of humor, a dash of spice,
Each sculpture laughed, oh so nice.
An odd-shaped lamp began to sing,
While dishes chimed in, doing their bling.

"Let's bake a laughter," shouted a dish,
"Fill it with giggles, that's my wish!"
With every twist of the potter's hand,
Crafted smiles scattered across the land.

The breath of art, a playful tease,
Brought life to clay with gentle ease.
Fingers play, in fun they bask,
Chasing joy is all we ask.

Glazes of Memory

In a shop of odd-shaped dreams,
Where clay dances in funny schemes.
A bowl spins, with glee it sways,
It tells tales from ancient days.

With glazes bright like candy sweets,
It wobbles on its little feet.
A mug with eyes that blink and cheer,
Laughs at the spills that draw it near.

A vase that sings when filled with blooms,
Whispers secrets in dusty rooms.
It once held soup, now it's a friend,
To all the laughter it can lend.

Oh, the joy in every crack,
Each chip brings stories on the track.
In every glaze, a memory sloshes,
In this world of ceramic splashes.

The Silence Between Shapes

In a realm where shadows dance,
There's a platter that takes a chance.
It sits in silence, bold and round,
Wonders why the world's so loud.

A teapot with a fancy hat,
Turns to gaze at a sleepy cat.
It suddenly spills a tale or two,
Of tea parties, and the oddest brew.

A jug with a neck so long and thin,
Claims it's the ruler of all within.
With every pour, it makes a sound,
Laughter ripples all around.

Behind each shape, secrets wait,
In this funny, ceramic fate.
With each silence, joy is near,
Crafted shapes that bring us cheer.

Handcrafted Harmonies

With hands that mold and hearts that sing,
A creature formed from clay takes wing.
A trumpet made of humble earth,
Plays a silly tune, for what it's worth.

A tiny cup that dreams of wine,
Wants to be fancy, seeks to shine.
It clinks and clatters on the shelf,
Wishes for parties, all by itself.

A bowl that giggles when it's full,
Says, "Life's a feast! It's never dull!"
As food flies by in perfect arcs,
It catches joy, like flying sparks.

In this workshop, laughter flows,
Crafting joy where humor grows.
Handcrafted tunes of every shape,
Make giggles bloom, a friendly drape.

Earthbound Elegies

In a garden of dust and clay,
A mug reminisces, come what may.
Its handle shaped like a funny grin,
Hopes for tales that never thin.

A plate adorned with lopsided joy,
Remembers the meals of a happy boy.
With laughter etched into each rim,
It dreams of picnics, sunlight's hymns.

A whimsical teapot pipes a tune,
Bubbles echo under the moon.
It jigs on the shelf, with playful flair,
Inviting teacups to comedy rare.

In the soil where stories dwell,
Every crafted piece has a tale to tell.
In earthbound elegies, laughter thrives,
Mirth and clay, where memory survives.

The Poetry Between Touch and Texture

In a kitchen alive with clinks and clatters,
A chef juggles spoons, oh, what silly matter!
Flour flies, like confetti from a party,
A pinch of chaos that feels quite hearty.

The pan's a canvas, sizzling with delight,
Eggs dancing frantically, what a sight!
Whisking up laughter, a sprinkle of fun,
Each meal's a poem when all's said and done.

Harmonies of Hearth and Hues

In cozy corners, shadows play around,
Bright colors shout, though silence is profound.
A quilt of laughter stitched with threads of cheer,
Each cozy night sings, 'Let's keep the fun near!'

The teapot whistles a rather loud tune,
While cookies frolic, oh, like balloons!
With every sip, a giggle is found,
In harmonies where joy is unbound.

Dreamscapes Carved in Generations

Grandma's tales, spun like yarn in the air,
Fables unfold with a comical flair.
Once a frog who dreamed of being a king,
Now leaps on the table, oh, the joy it can bring!

Spoons navigate stories like boats on a stream,
Each one a vessel for whimsy and dream.
What magic awaits in the deep, bubbling stew?
A banquet of laughter, both savory and new.

A Fabric of Words and Three-Dimensional Dreams

Words weave together, a tapestry bright,
Crafted in jest, with humor and light.
Fabric of dreams, sewn with stitches bold,
Every thread a giggle, every fold a gold.

In this world of whimsy, laughter's the seam,
Illuminating passions that sparkle and gleam.
With a flick of the wrist, tales come alive,
In a three-dimensional world where jesters thrive.

The Clay of Creation

In a workshop filled with dreams,
Silly shapes start sprouting seams.
Lumpy bowls or funny hats,
With wobbly legs and giggling spats.

A masterpiece? Well, sort of.
It's more of a muddled, messy love.
A vase that's half a teapot too,
Creativity's wild zoo!

Rolling out clay, a joyful mess,
The more I mold, the less I stress.
Pots that wobble, laugh and tease,
In my hands, they dance with ease.

So here's the joke, just take a glance,
This wonky piece leads to a dance.
With every curve, a chuckle grows,
My sculptor's heart, it simply flows.

Spirals in the Heart

Twisting and turning, what's that shape?
It could be art or a jolly cape!
A spiral pot, oh what a sight,
It's trying its best, to stand upright.

Corkscrew hearts and giggly lines,
Each curve a tale of silly designs.
It wobbles here, it wobbles there,
My spirals create a loving scare.

Spin it fast or spin it slow,
Watch it dance and put on a show.
With each swirl, laughter rings,
My clay sings of joyful things.

So when you see a pot askew,
Remember, it's made with love, it's true.
Finding joy in all that spins,
In every bloom, the laughter wins.

Phrases in the Ashes

In the kiln, things heat up high,
But keep your cool or you might cry!
Ashes speak, but listen close,
They whisper words that never doze.

A phrase like 'oops' finds its way,
On a mug that's meant for tea, not play.
Silly slogans, a face that's bright,
In smoky hues, they find delight.

'Burnt offerings' they all declare,
Laughter rises, fills the air.
For every pot that comes out wrong,
There's a tale of laughter, a playful song.

So here's to pots with phrases bold,
Stories of mishaps turned to gold.
In ashes, we find our greatest glee,
With every fire, we're free to be.

Shapes of Serendipity

Blobs and blobs from every mold,
Each odd shape, a story told.
A squiggle here, a puffball there,
My hands create what's beyond compare.

Who knew that art could be so fun?
With every flop, I've surely won.
A crooked vase or a silly cup,
Grab a brush, let's mix it up!

Serendipity, oh what a friend,
In every oops, we start to blend.
The beauty lies in what is wrong,
A quirky pot becomes a song.

So laugh with me through all that's made,
In every curve, let joy cascade.
For shapes that wobble bring pure delight,
In happy crafting, life feels right.

Sculpting Silence with Stanzas

In a quiet corner, a lump of clay,
The poet ponders what words to say.
With every poke and a playful squeeze,
He shapes the silence, as if to tease.

His fingers dance, a whimsical play,
Transforming mud in a comical way.
A wiggle here, and a twist just right,
A bowl emerges, much to his delight.

But then a bump, oh what a mess!
The bowl now wears a crooked dress!
With laughter loud, he takes a seat,
And writes a joke that can't be beat.

A pottery wheel spins with glee,
As words and clay find harmony.
In this absurdity, joy is found,
Creating smiles all around.

The Artisan's Song of Creation

An artist stands with a lump and grin,
What masterpiece will emerge from within?
He hums a tune, a jovial sound,
As visions of humor swirl all around.

A pinch of whimsy, a dash of fun,
A pot with a smile, oh, what a run!
He adds in a handle, then steps back wide,
That pot looks like it's trying to hide!

With every spin, the pot's getting high,
Like it might take off, oh my, oh my!
But with a plop, it lands back down,
The whole room erupts around the clown.

So laughter echoes as the clay transforms,
In this zany world where creativity warms.
The song of creation, a playful sway,
Bringing joy to all in the light of day.

Rhymes in the Tapestry of Clay

With clay in hand, a fun little game,
The poet thinks, 'This pot needs a name!'
He sculpts a thing with a wobbly base,
It looks like it's wearing a funny face.

Each curve and swirl, a jest well made,
A masterpiece born from a messy trade.
When asked what it's for, he shrugs and laughs,
'It holds divine thoughts or just some daft gaffs!'

He spins it round, a tornado flair,
Chasing ideas that float in the air.
The rhymes come pouring, from heart to hand,
A laughable twist in this whimsical land.

With every poke, the pot gives a shout,
'This poet's skills are in serious doubt!'
But giggles arise, as creations take flight,
In this dance with clay, all feels just right.

Crafting Breath into Terra Cotta

In fluffy slippers, he stomps with glee,
Creating wonders as funny as can be!
A squishy blob that resembles a beast,
'It's a pot!' he decides, and his laughter increased.

With a roll and a squish, he starts to sing,
To clay, he gives voice, a whimsical fling.
Each pot takes shape, with a funny quirk,
Like a party dancer, who just won't lurk.

His studio's filled with giggles and cheer,
As misshapen jars bring the world near.
But one pot sneezes, causing a ruckus,
It gallops away, making them chuckle and fuss.

Oh, joy in the mess, the splatter, the throw,
Clay laughter, endless, just seems to grow.
In crafting each piece, both humor and art,
Finding joy in the clay, straight from the heart.

The Craft of Connection

In the corner, a vessel spins,
High hopes and a cheeky grin.
Shaped like a fruit, but wobbly too,
It dreams of being famous, who knew?

A twist and a turn, it starts to lean,
Oops! There goes the only machine.
A splash of glaze, a dash of glee,
Artistry? Oh, that's just me!

The clay and the poet, both in dismay,
Arguing over who leads the way.
With laughter and lumps, what a delight,
They'll craft a connection by night.

So here's to the forms that giggle and sway,
Each gaffe is a part of the play.
In this muddy dance, we find our cheer,
Crafting connections, with no fear.

Fluid Forms and Fatalism

Mold it soft, watch it flow,
But beware of the heavy toe!
A tippy tip here, a wobble there,
Is it art, or just a nightmare?

In the depths of despair, a grin takes form,
A jug that resembles an unkempt swarm.
Who knew clay could come with such drama,
Looking like a sculpture from a telenovela?

Fate plays tricks, oh what a game,
Smashing the mold, but who is to blame?
A poet laughs, pouring tea from a mug,
While the clay on the wheel gives a joking shrug.

In the end the work is a sight to behold,
With stories of mishaps and adventures told.
Fluidity and fate in a comical dance,
Crafting a dream, given half a chance.

Clay Dreams and Verses

A dream in clay, or so it seems,
Shaped in visions, lost in dreams.
Rolling and squishing, oh what a game,
Making a pot that won't bring shame!

But wait! It slips, it's on the floor,
It splatted like a pancake, oh what a score!
Laughter bubbles, the poet chimes,
"A masterpiece in the making, just give it some time!"

The kiln is hot, spirits soar,
Can't wait to see what's in store!
An odd-shaped mug with a smiley face,
Brings warmth and cheer to any place.

With clay on hands and joy in our hearts,
Failed sculptures turn into quirky arts.
In this clay dance, life's little jest,
Every misstep is a funny fest.

Whispers in the Kiln

In the quiet of the kiln, whispers flutter,
About the mishaps, and the clatter.
Cups that giggle, vases that sigh,
What tales can pottery tell if you try?

A wobbly bowl with secrets to share,
It's jiggling and laughing without a care.
A poet wanders by, quill in hand,
To write of the mischief, oh isn't it grand?

Clay and ink, they form a bond,
Creating a chaos that goes far beyond.
As the heat rises, so do the jokes,
Artistry flourishes, amidst all the pokes.

So hear the kiln, with its giggly hum,
Of pots and poems, all mixed up and fun.
Laughter and folly, a glorious blend,
In the heart of creation, where friendships mend.

Strokes of a Clay Hand

With a pinch and a twirl, oh so grand,
A sculptor's dream in a clumsy hand.
Lopsided bowls that wobble and sway,
Each one a laugh, a joy to display.

I tried to create a vase tall and thin,
But it laughed so hard, it made me grin.
My masterpiece? It's more like a blob,
In my gallery of giggles, a real heartthrob.

The wheel spins quick, my head in a whirl,
As clay flings mockery, it gives me a twirl.
Laughter is molded with each round spin,
In this comical chaos, I joyfully win.

So here's to the art of mishaps and fun,
Where mistakes and humor are happily spun.
With each errant curve, a smile to embrace,
In the world of clay, we're all in our place.

Echoes of Earth and Ink

Scribbles and splats on a paper sheet,
Words take a dive, oh what a treat!
Ink spills like laughter, it runs and it rolls,
In this messy dance, creativity pulls.

The pen's a wild creature, it prances and plays,
Sketching silly sonnets in unpredictable ways.
A turtle in verse begins to race,
While elephants waltz in a joyous embrace.

Oh, hiccuping lines and stuttering dreams,
A chorus of chuckles unfurling like streams.
Each stanza a jester, each rhyme a surprise,
In this literary circus, imagination flies.

So let's toast to the madness, the playful delight,
To paper adventures, both silly and bright.
In the echoes of laughter, our stories are spun,
Creating a festival of ink — oh what fun!

Molding Thoughts under Fire

Under the flame, ideas ignite,
As I shape them with glee, pure delight.
A wonky teapot gives quite the frown,
It's the star of my show, a clay comedian's crown.

The heat makes me giggle, it warms up my soul,
As a wobbly cup takes on the role.
"Drink up!" it shouts in a voice oh so bold,
But spills out the tea — a twist to behold!

With each fiery jest, the clay starts to dance,
Under this pressure, it takes quite a chance.
A sturdy mug? More like a quirky friend,
In this chaotic studio, the fun never ends.

So here's to the kiln, where dreams come alive,
With laughter and warmth, oh how we thrive.
In the heat's embrace, let the silliness soar,
Molding thoughts with a chuckle, who could ask for more?

Verses from the Artisan's Heart

A bashful artist with paint in a swirl,
Crafting odd characters that giggle and twirl.
Each stroke a chuckle, each color a cheer,
In this whimsical world, nothing's austere.

A cat in a hat and a dog on a slide,
Dance through my canvas, oh what a ride!
They strut with such flair, it's a comical scene,
In this jolly jamboree, nothing is mean.

With a wink and a dash, my brushes take flight,
Creating a ruckus, a joyful sight.
Each line tells a joke, each hue whispers fun,
In the gallery of giggles, we laugh and run.

So here's to the art that tickles the soul,
With quirks and oddities that make us feel whole.
In this artisan heart, let the laughter impart,
For humor and joy are a beautiful art.

The Alchemy of Form and Thought

A clay mound sits, waiting for a hand,
With dreams of shape, it can't understand.
The sculptor grins with a mischievous cheer,
Twisting and turning with no hint of fear.

Ideas fly like butterflies in flight,
While muddy fingers revel in delight.
Each curve and edge brings a giggle, a laugh,
As the artist shapes a whimsical giraffe.

Laughter echoes amidst the dust,
As clay rebels, in play, it must.
A fantastic creature springs to life,
Made from a thought that once sparked strife.

In laughter, the vision starts to glow,
With each playful nudge and tender throw.
Pottery spins, a giggle in every turn,
For in this craft, our hearts shall yearn.

Tumbling Thoughts and Turning Clay

Thoughts tumble in a whirl like clay,
A funny dance where ideas sway.
Slip and slide, oh what a sight!
As hands play tricks both day and night.

The wheel spins fast, a joyful ride,
With quickened hands as thoughts collide.
A monster, a crown, or maybe a shoe,
Whatever it is, it's hard to construe.

Giggles escape with the splashes of mud,
Innocent chaos begins to flood.
With every twist, each playful shove,
This commotion, a creation of love.

At last, a thing of beauty stands proud,
Surrounded by laughter, cheers from the crowd.
With a wink and a nod, it's time to say,
Who knew such fun could come from this clay?

Alabaster Breaths and Muddy Lines

In this realm where laughter flows,
Lines of mud craft silly prose.
Alabaster dreams take flight,
Winging with giggles, pure delight.

The mix of white with earthy delight,
Produces creations that spark pure fright!
A cat with three eyes and no tail at all,
With every new model, we just can't help but sprawl.

Hands coated in joy, a mischievous grin,
As soggy thoughts find a way to begin.
A dance of imagination, nothing too serious,
Crafting the absurd, oh how delirious!

When all's complete, with a twinkle in eyes,
Pottery tells tales, beneath chuckling skies.
In mud, we find a playful embrace,
Creating laughter in this magical space.

Ceramics of the Soul

With each spin, my heart takes flight,
Crafting joy under soft moonlight.
Ceramics whisper secrets untold,
In a dance of laughter, bold and gold.

Jugans, mugs, or maybe a dish,
Each shape tells tales, fulfilling a wish.
Good humor flows through every pore,
Underneath laughter, we always crave more.

The soul's best canvas, so merry and bright,
Sharing chuckles, a pure delight.
Rolling the clay, we find our grace,
With hapless creations that giggle in place.

No frowning allowed in this playful space,
Where clay and heart freely embrace.
So let the world watch as we paint and sing,
In this silly realm, we are all queens and kings.

Sculpting Dreams with Earthly Ink

In a realm where clay meets jest,
A bard with his hands, oh what a test.
Molding shapes with giggles galore,
Each crack tells a joke, a funny lore.

Spinning tales on a wheel so round,
Laughter erupts without a sound.
A saucer becomes a hat with flair,
Who knew pottery could lead to dare?

With every lump and every squish,
The dreams take form, a playful wish.
A dragon flies, a cat now dances,
In the kiln of humor, true romance is.

So sculpt your dreams with muddy cheer,
For in these pots, we hold our beer!
A toast to laughter, to shapes divine,
In the artist's hands, oh how they shine!

Writing in the Dust of Creation

In a world of dust and cheeky grins,
The scribe begins where laughter spins.
With every swirl, stories arise,
From cheeky mice to giant pies.

Fingers dance on surfaces bare,
Sketching wonders with playful flair.
A castle made of crumbs and glee,
In this dusty realm, we're all so free.

Chasing tales through whirlwinds bright,
Unruly thoughts take flight each night.
Words tumble forth, like tumbleweeds,
In the atmosphere of silly deeds.

So let your ink be dust and fun,
A whimsical journey has just begun!
For in creation's airy bliss,
Risks and giggles go hand in fist!

Harmony of Fire and Expression

In the belly of the oven's roar,
The artist dreams, the flames explore.
With twinkling eyes, they dance around,
Creating magic, oh so profound.

Fingers covered in ash and glee,
Sculpting life, a fire spree.
A mug that giggles, a bowl that sings,
Crafted from turns and funny flings.

As pots are born from heavenly heat,
Laughter echoes, oh such a treat.
With every crackle, a tale spins wide,
In the warmth of jokes, our hearts abide.

So raise your glass, toast to the flame,
In the world of mirth, there's no shame!
For fire and laughter, hand in hand,
Bring forth creations that truly stand.

Textures of Time and Imagination

In the canvas of a timeless jest,
Textures weave, oh what a quest.
From bumpy roads to silky skies,
Each stroke a chuckle, each hue a surprise.

Layers peel back like an onion sweet,
Revealing tales beneath our feet.
A carpet spun from laughter's thread,
Where every whisper becomes widespread.

With crayons of joy, we sketch our fate,
Adventures unfolding, prompt and straight.
A spoon that stirs up dreams and schemes,
In this vibrant world, we chase our dreams.

So let imagination flow like wine,
In textures rich, our spirits align!
Creating funny moments with grace,
In this whimsical, art-filled space.

Stories Sprouting from a Kiln's Breath

From mud to mug, oh what a sight,
A lumpy lump escapes the night.
With a giggle and a twirl, it finds its grace,
A wobbly dance in a fired embrace.

The clay, it chuckles, with every spin,
As the potter grins with mischief within.
They shape a tale of laughter and fun,
A whimsical journey has just begun.

What shape is it now? Perhaps a hat?
Or maybe a vase for a friendly cat?
The kiln keeps secrets of every whim,
Each piece a story, each laugh a grin.

So gather 'round, come take a peek,
At the quirky wonders that clay can speak.
With joy and humor, they tell their fable,
Of spun and shaped, they're quite unstable!

The Warmth of Clay in Rhyme

Molding mud with hands so sly,
A squishy blob that wants to fly.
It wiggles, jiggles, full of cheer,
Creating chaos, let's give a cheer!

The potter laughs, oh what a mess,
This clay's a joker in a playful dress.
It lands like dough, on the floor with a sound,
As giggles erupt all around.

Each twirl of the wheel, a new surprise,
Shaping a monster, oh how it tries!
With eyes made of buttons and a funny nose,
It wobbles and jigs, in a dance it shows.

In every bake, a story's found,
Of laughter and fun, oh how it astounds!
With each sunny glaze and each drippy dip,
The warmth of clay brings joy on a trip.

Echoing Ballads of a Potter's Wheel

Around and around, the wheel goes 'round,
With clinks and clanks, a merry sound.
The clay sings softly, a quirky tune,
Spinning tall tales beneath the moon.

A lump transforms under hands so dear,
Creating chuckles, it draws us near.
With every curve, it shares a jest,
A jug or a goose, whatever's best.

It giggles with glee, as it takes its shape,
A vase or a mug, or a tall escape.
And the potter hums a whimsical song,
As laughter and clay, happily throng.

So when you see, a pot by chance,
Remember the jester, the clay's little dance.
For every piece tells of joys untold,
With echoing ballads, ancient and bold.

The Silent Marriage of Clay and Quill

Once upon a time, in a silent world,
Clay met a quill with ink unfurled.
Together they dreamed, of tales to spin,
Their laughter echoed, where fun begins.

The clay rolled a ball, with a wink and a smile,
While the quill scribbled doodles, going wild.
Creating a world, so oddly sweet,
Of pots and pens, where paper and earth meet.

It wrote of a mug that danced with glee,
While balancing tea on a wobbly knee.
The clay giggled back as it formed a grin,
A partnership, odd, yet filled with win.

So here's to the friends, who play day and night,
In a dance of creation, where joy is bright.
For every baked pot and every fine line,
Is a fusion of fun, oh how divine!

Threads of Mud and Metaphor

In a world of clay and jests,
Laughter spins like a wheel,
Each pot holds tales, no tests,
Wobbling dreams that reveal.

Muddy hands and silly rhymes,
Shape the nonsense we've found,
The art of slipping in times,
Where giggles are tightly bound.

With sassy glazes that gleam,
Each laugh a playful swirl,
Potter's heart makes the dream,
As mischief starts to twirl.

So let the wheel swiftly roll,
And jokes potently play,
For every clumsy control,
Turns mud into ballet.

Brews of Emotion and Earth

With each stir of soil and jest,
A brew of giggles, no mess,
Crafting cups of human zest,
Filled with chaos, I confess.

Swirling feelings in the clay,
Make it steep in laughter's way,
Brewed connections day by day,
Ears to secrets pots convey.

Each sip a smirk, each gulp a grin,
Life's joy poured without a fin,
Sipping on what's held within,
A shared chuckle, let's begin.

Filled with warmth like the sun's ray,
Crafted spirals make hearts sway,
In every vessel, come what may,
Here blooms laughter, bright as day.

Silenced Songs of Stoneware

In the corner, pots are shy,
Hiding songs beneath the rim,
With every quirk, they amplifying,
A serenade that's doomed to dim.

But once they hear the jester's call,
They rattle and roll, oh what a brawl!
With clay and giggles sounding tall,
No song too humble, no laugh too small.

In their silence, tales concealed,
Of clownish pots that never yield,
In every crack, a jest revealed,
Where humor and warmth are sealed.

So let me tap on this old glaze,
To wake the songs from their haze,
A pot that laughs in funny ways,
Turns mundane to vibrant praise.

Vessel for Verse

In a world of clay concocted,
Verses spin like tops in play,
With pots that giggle, slightly rocked,
Holding stories, bright and fey.

Each vessel's rim a playful smile,
Belly-bouncing rhymes that flow,
Sipping joy, it takes a while,
To fill the soul with all that glow.

The heart of the artist beats with glee,
Creating bowls, bizarre and hearty,
Every chip a memory, see?
In laughter, clay becomes a party.

So raise your cup, let laughter rise,
A vessel's charm, a pot's disguise,
In humor's grasp, we find the prize,
With joyful grins and merry sighs.

Rhymes in the Mold

In a studio, clay flies with glee,
Laughter bubbles like hot chamomile tea.
Mistakes turn to magic, what a delight,
Mold it like putty, keep it light!

Fingers covered in goo, what a sight,
Chasing the mischief that dances in flight.
Silly shapes emerge, a curious blend,
Who knew a cup could also be a friend?

With a wink and a twist, I sculpt my rhymes,
Juggling my puns, committing no crimes.
Each curve and swirl, a jest to behold,
Creating more tales in the forms that unfold.

So here's to the fun of creating each day,
Even if my cup looks like a stray bouquet!
With laughter in lines and joy in the fold,
These rhymes in the mold are more precious than gold.

Shadows in the Studio

Shadows are dancing, the lights flicker low,
With every mishap, more laughter does grow.
A canvas of clay, a vision in flight,
Each slip of my hand leads to pure delight.

The glaze goes on thick, what could go wrong?
A pot looks like breakfast—more silly than strong!
I smile at the chaos, embrace every flaw,
A masterpiece born from a moment of 'Whoa!'

A sudden collision, oh dear, what's the fuss?
My sculpture's a monster, or perhaps a bus?
Laughter erupts like clay on the floor,
Art isn't perfection, it's laughter galore!

With shadows as friends, I smile at the mess,
In this studio chaos, I find my success.
So here's to creating with heart and with cheer,
For in every shadow, good humor draws near.

Sculpting Stanzas

With a pinch and a poke, I craft with delight,
Sculpting my stanzas, they take off in flight.
A lump of plain clay becomes full of cheer,
Turning words into shapes that tickle the ear.

Each line is a coil, I stack them with flair,
A whimsical tower reaching high in the air.
Oh, what a journey, from thought to a groove,
Laughter erupts as the figures all move!

I mold silly phrases, a tip here and there,
Blending humor with clay, I make quite the pair.
As the kiln starts to heat, my worries unwind,
In sculpting my stanzas, pure joy is defined.

With every small crumble, I chuckle out loud,
For these silly creations, I'm endlessly proud.
So here's to the quirks, the art and the craft,
In sculpted stanzas, true joy is the draft.

Fire's Embrace

In the fire's warm glow, my worries ignite,
With pots doing funny dances, oh what a sight!
I chuckle and grin, as they twist and they turn,
For in fiery chaos, there's so much to learn.

A mishap with glaze—what a colorful splash,
My masterpiece's look—like a comical crash.
But as I peer closely, I see through the haze,
Each blunder and blob brings a laugh to amaze.

The flames crackle loudly, like laughter in air,
As creations emerge, I find joy everywhere.
With each playful piece, I take in the warmth,
Art in the fire—what a whimsical charm!

So here's to the magic of things that we make,
In flames of amusement, let's celebrate and quake.
For art isn't perfect, it's a joyous exchange,
In the fire's embrace, I find laughter strange.

Silent Words

In quiet reflections, the clay starts to speak,
With hints of humor, it's quite the unique.
No need for loud chatter; just shapes hold the key,
To unlock all the laughter that's hidden in me.

Each curve tells a tale, a giggle or two,
Silly whispers and puns, they bubble right through.
A fistful of thoughts, so playful, so sly,
These silent words dance, and they just can't lie!

Molding with glee, my hands create sound,
As the soft clay giggles and stretches around.
Every pinch and each squish shares laughter and fun,
Crafting a statue, a jester on the run.

So here's to communications of a funny kind,
Where silence brings smiles and joy intertwined.
These silent words, they play in a soft hue,
In the art of creation, it's laughter that's true.

Shaping Stories in Ceramics

In a workshop, a lump sat still,
Dreaming of forms both strange and shrill.
A sculptor laughed, took it in hand,
Twisting and turning, oh what a grand!

With some giggles, and quite a mess,
A mug emerged, quite absurd, I confess.
It had ears like a cat, a nose like a pig,
The old artist chuckled, now that's quite big!

Yet who could sip from this silly brew?
A clown with a smile perhaps, just for you!
Each curve tells a tale, each color a jest,
In this land of clay, we're truly blessed!

So if you find pots shaped in glee,
Remember the hands that molded so free.
Laughter and clay, a perfect embrace,
In the heart of the kiln, we find our place.

A Dance of Clay and Word

Once a ball of clay rolled around,
It toppled and stumbled, then fell to the ground.
A poet nearby couldn't resist,
"Let's shape this silliness," he wittily hissed!

With a twist and a turn, like a dance on the floor,
The poet declared, "Let's make it a door!"
But the clay had a mind, it sought a new craze,
"Why not a hat instead? I fancy some praise!"

The sculptor chuckled, the words did collide,
"Your hat is too funny!" As the giggles abide.
With vases that dance and bowls that sing,
They created a world where clay wore a bling!

So laugh with your vessels, let words take their lead,
In the dance of the clay, let your heart be freed.
For in this ballet, where stories combine,
We craft our own joy, one rhyme at a time.

The Alchemy of Earth and Emotion

From mud and giggles, some magic's begun,
A pot with wild laughter, oh so much fun!
It bubbled and wobbled, with joy it did shine,
A masterpiece born from whimsy divine!

A poet stood watching, tickling the clay,
"Let's make it a teapot that dances today!"
It sprang into action, with spout and with lid,
"Oh look, it's now laughing!" they both wildly kid!

This teapot of joy filled with stories so bright,
Leaps from the table in pure delight!
In the heart of creation, they found a new scheme,
As clay turned to laughter, they lived in a dream!

So gather your laughter, your heart, and your cheer,
In the alchemy of art, let whimsy draw near.
For earth and emotion, in playful embrace,
Bring joy to the world, with a smile on your face.

Fragments of Legend in Porcelain

In a kingdom of clay, legends twirled,
Mugs with mustaches, what a sight unfurled!
A lad with a grin, crafted tales of old,
With jugs and with jars, their secrets unfold.

"Once upon a time," he would chirp with delight,
"A teacup took flight in the soft, starry night!"
The audience giggled, their spirits so high,
As a bowl told a tale of a pie in the sky.

With shards of bright colors, the stories took shape,
A platter, a cup, a whimsical grape!
Each piece held a dream and danced with a spin,
In the realm of porcelain, where laughter begins!

So raise up your vessels, toast to the jest!
In fragments of legend, we find we're all blessed.
For in every pot lies a tale yet to hear,
In the laughter of clay, we banish our fear.

Echoing Memories in Fired Earthenware

Once a bowl, round and stout,
Chasing dreams, there's no doubt.
It holds soup and silly jokes,
Echoing laughter of clumsy folks.

From the shelf, it takes a leap,
In the air, its secrets seep.
What careens, now makes a splash,
Faded past, in a messy crash.

All the tales from meals once shared,
Morsels sweet and those that scared.
With every chip, a story spills,
Laughter's found among the thrills.

So here's to bowls, their merry fate,
Collecting joy while they wait.
In their curves, we find delight,
A porcelain party, through day and night.

The Shape of Words in a Clay Vessel

Words like dough, they twist and turn,
In a mold, they rise and yearn.
A phrase plopped, then stretched so wide,
Watch it wobble, giggle inside.

With a poke and a careful spin,
Each letter shaped to make us grin.
They dance around in playful glee,
Baking stories for you and me.

A pinch of wit, a sprinkle of rhyme,
Mixing potions for fun each time.
Here's a goblet of silly thoughts,
Chasing chuckles, connecting dots.

In the kiln, they warm with cheer,
Each quirky tale, a souvenir.
Raise your cup, let laughter roll,
Words shaped well, nourish the soul.

Patterns of Life in Shaping Hands

Hands that shape a merry crew,
With clay, they play, and play some more too.
They sculpt the past, the silly bits,
Laughter logs, and life's little skits.

From fingertips to messy palms,
Creating fun, amid the qualms.
Each swirl tells a story's twist,
Artsy antics that can't be missed.

With every press and loving knead,
A whimsical world, we plant the seed.
In wet earth, we plant our dreams,
Shaping smiles, or so it seems.

So let's embrace our crafted fate,
As hands rejoice and celebrate.
In this pottery of life we tread,
All the patterns that joy has spread.

Prose and Porcelain Intertwined

Prose finds home in porcelain bliss,
A saucer's edge, a writer's kiss.
Words dribble like tea in cups,
Spilling tales of joyful pups.

Each sip of tea, a story sipped,
Writing tales while the world has tripped.
Chasing ideas 'round the rim,
In delicate dance, with a silly whim.

The clink of china, a writer's cheer,
Puns afloat, as laughter draws near.
Characters swirl in perfect glaze,
With porcelain laughs, they set ablaze.

So raise your cup, let giggles fly,
Crafting fun, oh me, oh my!
Prose and pots, a quirky blend,
In the echo of giggles, they never end.

Inked Whispers Tailored in Clay

A vessel sits with dreams in tow,
Its dance begins, a charming show.
With scribbles bright and colors bold,
A merry tale of clay is told.

But when the ink meets pottery,
A grand confusion, oh, what glee!
The poet laughs, the potter grins,
In laughter's game, the fun begins.

Versatility of Earth

Round and squishy, oh what fun,
Shaped for laughs, it's never done.
A mug for tea or bowl for stew,
Each curve a twist, a laugh anew.

The earth can sculpt both thick and thin,
While words of wit bring grins within.
A pun or two, then watch them fly,
As clay and verse both reach the sky.

Richness of Words

Words swirl like clay, soft and slick,
A chuckle here, a playful trick.
With each new verse, a pot takes shape,
Something lovely, a verbal drape.

Laughter echoes as the pot does spin,
Each word like glaze, where fun begins.
Rich hues of humor coat each line,
In this pot, each joke does shine.

A Journey in Shape and Sonnet

Oh, twist and turn as potters do,
Each spin a chance for something new.
Melodies hum, as hands awake,
A sonnet born from a soft break.

In double meanings, laughter grows,
One line a pun, each stanza flows.
With clay in hand and cheer in heart,
Every crafted piece, a work of art.

Ephemeral Forms

A clay creation, bright and bold,
Holds secrets of the tales we've told.
Though forms may fade, the laughter stays,
In every nook, a joke always plays.

Time ticks on, but don't you fret,
Each silly shape, we won't forget.
A wink, a nod; the pot recalls,
The laughter shared in playful stalls.

Lasting Lines

Lines etched in clay, a quirky plight,
Frame our whims in the morning light.
Each chuckle shaped, each smile cast,
With every twist, the shadows last.

In playful rhymes, our stories blend,
From potter's wheel to page, they mend.
So raise a cup, let's toast tonight,
To clay and verse, a pure delight.

Shaping the Unsayable in Clay

With every spin upon the wheel,
I tell a tale, yet keep it real.
My hands are messy, oh what a sight,
But pot-shaped treasures bring pure delight.

I miss the mark, my bowl looks wry,
A lopsided cup that won't hold dry.
I'll call it art, with a cheeky grin,
Who knew my clay could wear such sin?

A jug for tea, or maybe a shoe,
My kiln's confused, it can't know what's true.
In every fracture, a story hides,
I laugh aloud as chaos collides.

So raise a toast to every blunder,
In every mishap, there's magic under.
For when I shape and start to play,
I find pure joy in this clay-mad way.

Whispers of Love in Glazed Stories

In a workshop dim, with glazes around,
I craft sweet whispers, soft and profound.
A heart-shaped dish, that's now quite the joke,
For love served here may cause a stroke.

The spouts of teapots, they giggle at night,
Their stories of love are silly and light.
A dip in the glaze, a splash of the soul,
My cup runneth over, it's really a stroll.

A mug for coffee, or maybe for soup,
With each little misfire, I dance with the group.
What's that? A crack? Oh, make it a scene,
"Unique" is the phrase that I love to mean!

So let's raise our mugs, all mismatched and bright,
To love in the clay, with laughter in sight.
For every chip tells tales of our cheer,
In glazed stories, we sip on the dear.

Rebirth of Clay and Heart's Ink

With each knead and pinch, I feel reborn,
My heart's ink flows where dreams are worn.
I sculpt my wishes, they wiggle with glee,
Oh, what a sight—a wobbly jubilee!

A vase for a flower; it fell on its nose,
Yet, laughter erupts where every clay grows.
Each swirl and each twirl bears no perfect line,
Just a mud-splattered love, truly divine.

So here's to the vessel that never stays still,
Embracing each curve, I dance with a thrill.
In every mistake, there's a quirky delight,
A heart filled with laughter, it feels just right.

For clay is a canvas, and I am the brush,
Creating a world where we giggle and hush.
In this playful ride of mud and ink swell,
I find every fault just fits like a spell.

Sensations Etched in Soft Earth

The earth beneath laughs, it knows all my tricks,
With every soft pat, I'm building my mix.
A whimsy of shapes, what will next emerge?
A snail or a cat? Oh, feel the urge!

I press my palms in, a dimple of fate,
What's this I've made? A bowl that's not straight!
But in every curve lies a tale of my heart,
Where giggles and blunders collide as an art.

So let's toast the shapes that cannot stay still,
Each curve, each line, floods my spirit with thrill.
In this playground of clay, I'll dance through the muck,
With laughter as clay; who needs any luck?

For every mishap is a moment to cheer,
In soft earth I find my joy, my dear.
Let the wheels spin wild, let the laughter take flight,
In this clay-crafting tale, everything feels right.

The Narrative of a Singed Edge

In clay they met, a mismatched pair,
The artist's whim, the vessel's dare.
With every twist, a laugh resounds,
As fire crackles, joy abounds.

A splash of color, a dash of flair,
The pot was wild, with nooks laid bare.
The poet scribbled, chuckles in tow,
A masterpiece made from the woe.

Glimmers and glazes, what a sight,
The pot demanded, 'Make me bright!'
Yet in the chaos, poetry grew,
With every blunder, a quip anew.

So here's to the dance, the funny plight,
Of malleable dreams in creative flight.
For in the kiln's warmth, laughter stays,
In the tale of two, a snicker displays.

Artistry Born from the Earth

In mud so rich and full of jest,
The maker laughed, he felt so blessed.
With hands all messy, ideas swirl,
Creating forms where giggles twirl.

Oh, the clay rebelled, it didn't obey,
It squished and squashed, in silly play.
The thrown pot wobbled, then had a fit,
While the poet scribbled, humor lit.

Each bump and curve a tale to tell,
As laughter echoed where clay would dwell.
A work of art, with cracks so bright,
Comedy shines in the morning light.

Nature's magic mixed with glee,
In every mound, a jest, you see.
From earth and rhyme, the fabric spun,
A wacky dance where art's begun.

A Canvas of Nature and Nurture

Beneath the sun, the artist grinned,
With soil and laughter, his joy pinned.
He shaped a pot, a wonky sight,
Nature chuckled, "Oh what a fright!"

A splash of dirt, a daub of cheer,
The vase looked up and cried, "I'm here!"
While petals laughed, their colors bold,
A floral dance in stories told.

With quill in hand, the poet played,
Each scribbled line, a joke displayed.
As vines entwined in comedic plots,
They stammered softly, "Why not? Why not?"

Together they spun a wobbly tale,
With nature's paint and giggly hail.
In clay they crafted more than a piece,
A canvas of laughter that would not cease.

Chiseled Memories

With hammer thuds and grins so wide,
The sculptor sought what joy couldn't hide.
A chip here, a skip there, oh what fun,
As memories laughed under the sun.

The stone would grin, though quite annoyed,
"Do you think I'm just a tool, deployed?"
While the poet snickered at the rock's retort,
"Chiseled dreams? Let's make them short!"

Each crack, a chuckle, each line, a tease,
As artistry sprang with effortless ease.
A comedy carved from stubborn heft,
In every stroke, laughter was left.

So here's a toast to the art we wield,
With silly thoughts and soft hearts revealed.
For in the craft, where stone meets the jest,
Chiseled memories put humor to the test.

Textured Rhymes

In fibers woven with quirky flair,
The poet found a style quite rare.
With textured lines and patterns bold,
Each verse unveiled a laugh to hold.

A tapestry spun with a giggly twist,
The fabric teased, "You can't resist!"
The potter waved a wand of clay,
With every shape, a funny display.

Stitches of humor, a patchwork song,
In every seam where the chuckles belong.
As text transformed in colors so bright,
They spun together in pure delight.

So let the threads of laughter blend,
In artistry where nonsense won't end.
For every texture, each rhyme so free,
A joyful dance in creativity.

www.ingramcontent.com/pod-product-compliance
Lightning Source LLC
Chambersburg PA
CBHW072116070526
44585CB00016B/1474